# Home and School

## Writing Skills
## Book A

Angela Redfern

Folens Publishers

# Introduction

## The value of homework

Homework is a very successful means of providing children with the opportunity to consolidate skills taught in the classroom. It is also a way of providing parents or carers with a practical means of participating in their children's education. It used to be thought that helping children was somehow 'cheating' and that a child should undertake any homework without any consultation with parents. The advent of the Parents' Charter has encouraged parents to play a much more active part in supporting their children's learning. Homework is an ideal means of providing a clear role for parental participation.

Teachers recognise the need for children to spend further time on skills that they have introduced in the classroom. The curriculum demands on time, however, rarely allow for this revisiting. Homework offers some children the opportunity to work undisturbed for an extended period of time – a situation that is difficult for the teacher to provide regularly in the classroom.

## Developing writing

In order for children to acquire the high level of literacy that society demands they need to be able to express themselves clearly, spell correctly and write in a legible handwriting style. Parents or carers can play a crucial role in helping their children to master these skills. By working hand in hand with the school they can offer support and encouragement and provide much needed practice in a range of writing activities.

## Components of this book

### Teachers' notes

This book is divided into seven sections, each covering a different aspect of spelling, grammar, handwriting and presentation. An introductory page precedes each section. Here, each activity is described in detail with advice to the teacher on how to set up the homework.

### Activity sheets

At the bottom of each activity sheet there are clear instructions to the carer and child. The 'From the teacher' box explains the main purpose of the activity and offers suggestions as to how parents or carers could support their children. The teacher is encouraged to add to, or omit information from this box to suit the needs of the individual pupil. The 'To the teacher' box is included for the parent or carer to sign and date after their child has completed the activity.

### Homework diary

Pages 46–7 are designed to be put together to form a homework diary. Brief advice to the parent or carer is written on the back cover.

### Organisation of the series

The three books in this series offer a homework series for children from 4–7 years. Each book builds upon the content of the previous book so that progression and continuity are assured and this enables teachers to select the most appropriate activities for the children in their class.

Editor: Hayley Willer    Layout artist: James Brown    Illustrations: Kim Woolley    Title page: Claire Boyce – Graham-Cameron Illustration
Cover image: Karen Tushingham – Mundys' Illustration Agency    Cover design: John Hawkins

© 1997 Folens Limited, on behalf of the author.
Every effort has been made to contact copyright holders of material used in this book. If any have been overlooked, we will be pleased to make any necessary arrangements.

British Library Cataloguing in Publication Data. A catalogue record for this book is available from the British Library.

First published 1997 by Folens Limited, Dunstable and Dublin.
Folens Limited, Albert House, Apex Business Centre, Boscombe Road, Dunstable, LU5 4RL, England.

ISBN 1 85276 381-7

Printed in Singapore by Craft Print.

# Contents

# Handwriting patterns – Teachers' notes

## Introduction

*These activities will help to promote good handwriting habits. Children should be encouraged to hold their pencil in a comfortable position and to complete the patterns in one flowing movement from left to right, starting at the top of the page. They should say aloud what they are doing. This approach means that they see, hear and feel the movement across the page. A few children may need an adult to guide their hand; most will need to write over the patterns with crayons, highlighters or fingers several times to get the feel of the movement into the hand; some may be able to copy the patterns without difficulty. Children with well-developed fine motor skills can decorate their work with borders of handwriting patterns.*

## Make it look like a rug
### (Zigzag patterns)

**Aim:** To practise the pattern so that the movement becomes relaxed and automatic.
**Activity:** The child should work with an adult. They should say together: "Start at the dot, follow the arrows and go down, up, down, up, down, up." This pattern prepares the hand for writing the letters: **v w**.

## Make it look like a towel
### (Straight line patterns)

**Aim:** To practise writing short straight lines in one movement with confidence.
**Activity:** The child should work with an adult. They should say together: "Start at the dot, follow the arrow and go along, along, along. Start at the dot, follow the arrow and go down, down, down." This pattern prepares the hand for writing the letters: **x z**.

## Waves
### (Wave patterns)

**Aim:** To practise the pattern in a comfortable flowing movement from left to right across the page, without lifting the pencil until the end of the line is reached.
**Activity:** The child should work with an adult. They should say together: "Start at the dot, follow the arrows and go down, round and up, down, round and up." This pattern prepares the hand for writing the letters: **i u y j l t**.

## Make it look like a tablecloth
### (Arch patterns)

**Aim:** To practise the pattern in a comfortable flowing movement from left to right across the page, without lifting the pencil until the the end of the line is reached.
**Activity:** The child should work with an adult. They should say together: "Start at the dot, follow the arrows and go down, up and over, down, up and over." This pattern prepares the hand for writing the letters: **r n m h b p**.

## Make it look like a quilt
### (Round shapes)

**Aim:** To practise writing round shapes in an anticlockwise direction so that the movement becomes relaxed and automatic.
**Activity:** The child should work with an adult. They should say together: "Start at the dot and follow the arrow all the way round." This pattern prepares the hand for writing the letters: **o a d c e g q**.

**Name:** _____

# Make it look like a rug

● Draw a pattern on the rug. As you write say: "Start at the dot, follow the arrows and go down, up, down, up." Try not to lift your pencil until you reach the end of the line.

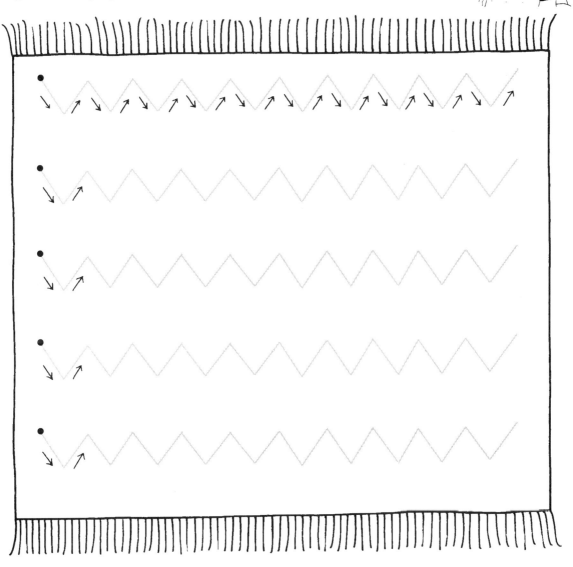

● On the back of this sheet, decorate another rug with a 'down, up' pattern.

**From the teacher**
Please read this sheet with your child. The activity helps children to learn to write from left to right in one flowing movement, starting at the top of the page. The pattern prepares the hand for writing the letters: **v w**.

**To the teacher**

Signed: _____

Date: _____

HOME AND SCHOOL – *Writing Skills: Book A*    5

Name: _____

# Make it look like a towel

- Draw a pattern on the beach towel. As you write say: "Start at the dot, follow the arrow and go along, along, along." Lift your pencil at the end of each straight line.

| → | → | → | → |
|---|---|---|---|
| → | → | → | → |
| → | → | → | → |
| → | → | → | → |
| → | → | → | → |
| → | → | → | → |

- Now draw a pattern on this beach towel, saying aloud: "Start at the dot, follow the arrow and go down, down, down."

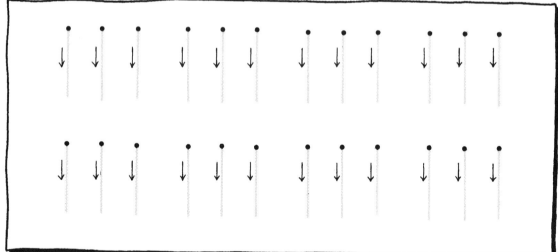

- On the back of this sheet, draw another beach towel with straight line patterns.

**From the teacher**
Please read this sheet with your child. The activity helps children to write short straight lines in one movement with confidence. The pattern prepares the hand for writing the letters: **x z**.

**To the teacher**

Signed: _____

Date: _____

**Name:** _____

# Waves

● Finish the waves. As you write say: "Start at the dot, follow the arrows and go down, round and up, down, round and up." Try not to lift your pencil until you reach the end of the line.

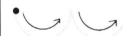

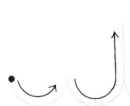

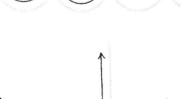

● On the back of this sheet, design some clothes with wave patterns.

**From the teacher**
Please read this sheet with your child. The activity helps children to write from left to right in one flowing movement. The pattern prepares the hand for writing the letters: **i u y j l t**.

**To the teacher**

Signed: _____

Date: _____

**Name:** _____

# Make it look like a tablecloth

● Draw a pattern on the tablecloth. As you write say: "Start at the dot, follow the arrows and go down, up and over, down, up and over." Try not to lift your pencil until you reach the end of the line.

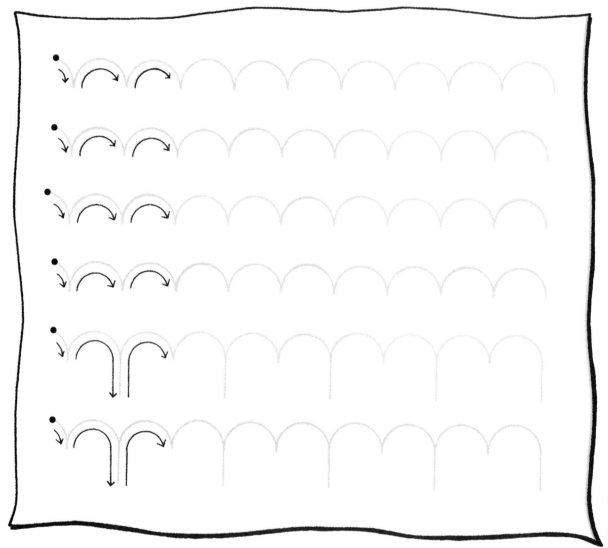

● On the back of this sheet, design some cushions and curtains with arch patterns.

**From the teacher**
Please read this sheet with your child. The activity helps children to write from left to right in one flowing movement across the page. The pattern prepares the hand for writing the letters: **r n m h b p**.

**To the teacher**

Signed: _____

Date: _____

**Name:** _____

# Make it look like a quilt

- Draw a pattern on the quilt. As you write say: "Start at the dot and follow the arrow all the way round." Lift your pencil after finishing each round shape.

- On the back of this sheet, design some pillowcases and sheets with round shapes.

# Letter formation – Teachers' notes

## Introduction
*These activities will help children to recognise, name and write lower-case letters. They should be shown where to start and finish each letter and be told the letter names as they write. Check that the pencil grip is relaxed and encourage:*
- *'flicks' for appropriate letters, ready for joining letters later on*
- *clear ascenders and descenders*
- *the children to say aloud what they are doing.*

*Point out similarities and differences between the letters in the same group and encourage the children to make comparisons as well as to look for letters that occur in their own name.*

---

**Page 11**

### Headbands
### (The letters: v w x z )

**Aims:**
- To provide practice in the correct formation of the letters: **v w x z**.
- To increase competence and confidence, and to raise awareness of the English alphabet.

**Activity:** The child should work with an adult and write each letter in one flowing movement.

---

**Page 12**

### Scarves
### (The letters: i u l t y j )

**Aims:**
- To provide practice in the correct formation of the letters: **i u l t y j**.
- To increase competence and confidence, and to raise awareness of the English alphabet.
- To encourage the inclusion of a 'flick' for the letters: **i u l t**.

**Activity:** The child should work with an adult and write each letter in one flowing movement.

---

**Page 13**

### Ribbons
### (The letters: r n m h b p )

**Aims:**
- To provide practice in the correct formation of the letters: **r n m h b p**.
- To increase competence and confidence, and to raise awareness of the English alphabet.
- To encourage the inclusion of a 'flick' for the letters: **n m h**.

**Activity:** The child should work with an adult and write each letter in one flowing movement.

---

**Page 14**

### Belts
### (The letters: a c e d g q )

**Aims:**
- To provide practice in the correct formation of the letters: **a c e d g q**.
- To increase competence and confidence, and to raise awareness of the English alphabet.
- To encourage the inclusion of a 'flick' for the letters: **a e c d**.

**Activity:** The child should work with an adult and write each letter in one flowing movement.

---

**Page 15**

### Worms, slugs and lizards
### (The letters: s f k )

**Aims:**
- To provide practice in the correct formation of the letters: **s f k**.
- To increase competence and confidence, and to raise awareness of the English alphabet.

**Activity:** The child should work with an adult and write each letter in one flowing movement. If you prefer to introduce alternative ways of writing **k** and **s**, you will need to adapt the sheet accordingly.

**Name:** _____

# Headbands

● Draw a pattern on each headband. Start at the dot and follow the arrows.

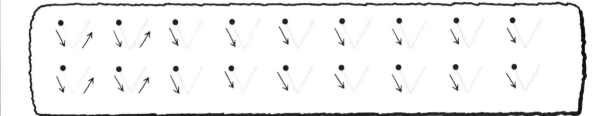

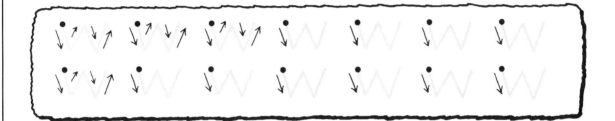

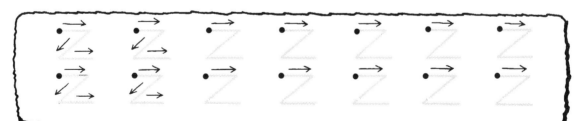

● Look through books and magazines and find some words that contain these letters. Write ten of the words on the back of this sheet.

**From the teacher**
Please read this sheet with your child. The activity helps children to form correctly and confidently the letters: **v w x z**.

**To the teacher**

Signed: _____

Date: _____

**Name:** _____

# Scarves

● Write over the letters on the scarves. Start at the dot and follow the arrows.

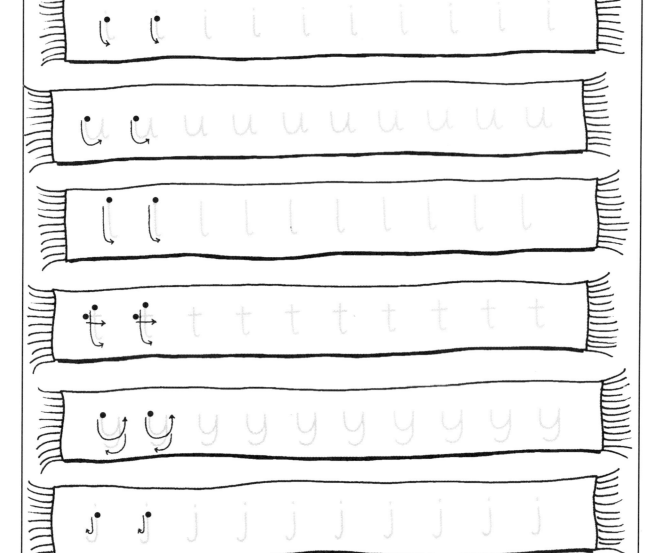

● Look at street signs, adverts and shop signs and find some words that contain these letters. Write ten of the words on the back of this sheet.

**Name:** _____

# Ribbons

● Write over the letters on the ribbons. Start at the dot and follow the arrows.

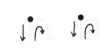

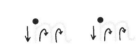

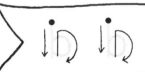

● On the back of this sheet make a list of the names of all the people you know. Look for these letters in their names and underline them.

**From the teacher**
Please read this sheet with your child. The activity helps children to write confidently and correctly the letters: **r n m h b p**. Ask your child to comment on the similarities and differences between these letters.

**To the teacher**

Signed: _____

Date: _____

**Name:** _____

# Belts

● Write over the letters on the belts. Start at the dot and
follow the arrows. Complete each letter in one movement.

● Make a list of your favourite television programmes.
Look for the above letters in your list and underline them.

**From the teacher**
Please read this sheet with your child. The activity helps children to
write confidently and correctly, in one flowing movement, the letters:
**a c e d g q**. Ask your child to comment on the similarities and differences
between these letters.

**To the teacher**

Signed: _____

Date: _____

HOME AND SCHOOL – *Writing Skills: Book A*

**Name:** _____

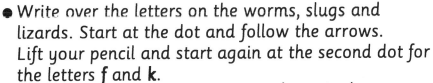

# Worms, slugs and lizards

● Write over the letters on the worms, slugs and lizards. Start at the dot and follow the arrows. Lift your pencil and start again at the second dot for the letters **f** and **k**.

● Decorate the wriggly worms.

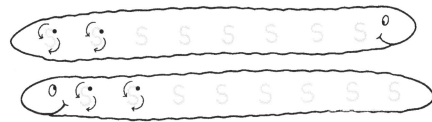

● Decorate the slimy slugs.

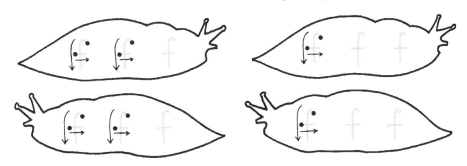

● Decorate the lazy lizards.

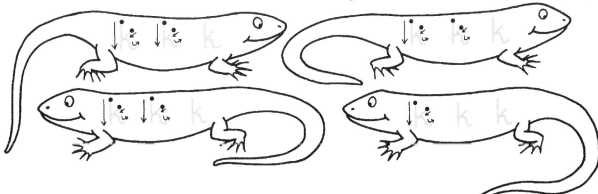

● Look through some books and comics and find some words that contain these letters. Write ten of the words on the back of this sheet.

**From the teacher**
Please read this sheet with your child. The activity helps children to write confidently and correctly the letters: **s f k**. These letters are difficult to write so be patient!

**To the teacher**

Signed: _____

Date: _____

# Capital letters – Teachers' notes

## Introduction

*These activities will help children to:*

- *recognise, name and write capital letters*
- *know that capital letters are used for the names of people and products*
- *recognise and write the words that they use frequently in their personal stories and which occur in their home or school environment.*

*Many children will need to trace over an adult's writing; some children may wish to copy underneath an adult's writing; a few children may wish to make their own marks on paper. Some children may be able to make associations between the initial letters and sounds in names and known words.*

### My name
### (Writing own name)

**Page 17**

**Aim:** To consolidate correct letter formation, and to help children to recognise and write their own name confidently and accurately.

**Activity:** This can be linked with classroom activities which encourage children to compare names:

- Which is the longest/shortest?
- Which ones start with the same letter?
- Which have repeats of the same letters?
- Which have double letters?
- Which have all different letters?

### My initial
### (Writing own initial)

**Page 18**

**Aim:** To reinforce the use of capital letters for proper nouns and to help children to recognise the initial capital letter of their own name.

**Activity:** This can be linked with classroom activities to promote alphabet awareness, for instance making alphabet books of names of real, famous or fictitious characters. It can also be linked to classroom activities to promote phonological awareness. For example, nursery rhymes involving names – Jack and Jill, Polly Flinders and Dr Foster could be highlighted.

### My family
### (Family names)

**Page 19**

**Aim:** To recognise and write correctly and confidently the words for family relationships that occur in most early reading books and which children use frequently in their own early writing.

**Activity:** This can be linked with classroom activities on family trees as well as with bookmaking activities centred on, for instance, 'Me and my family'.

### My friends
### (Friends' names)

**Page 20**

**Aim:** To develop awareness of initial capital letters, English names and names in other cultures.

**Activity:** This will help children to write correctly and confidently the names of people that they use frequently in their own stories. It also offers the opportunity to talk about similarities and differences between names.

### My favourite food
### (Labelling food)

**Page 21**

**Aim:** To write correctly and confidently the product names of foods – words with which the children come into daily contact.

**Activity:** This will reinforce work done in school on letter formation, the alphabet and phonological awareness. Some children will enjoy playing guessing games based on the alphabet. For example, I am thinking of something to eat that begins with the letter **W**. Some children will enjoy playing guessing games based on letter sounds. For example, I am thinking of a food beginning with the sound **p** (pizza).

**Name:** _____

# My name

● Write your name on the badges below and say each letter aloud as you write.
Do not forget to start with a capital letter!

**From the teacher**
Please read this sheet with your child. The activity helps children to write their names correctly and with confidence. Tell your child that we use capital letters at the start of names of people, places and products.

**To the teacher**

Signed: _____

Date: _____

**Name:** _____

# My initial

● Draw the first letter of your name.
  Colour it with felt-tipped pens or crayons.
  Cut it out carefully.
  Stick a piece of cotton or string to the back of it
  with sticky tape to make a mobile for your bedroom.

**From the teacher**
Read this sheet with your child. The activity helps children to recognise capital letters. Remind your child that capital letters
are used for the names of people, places and products.

HOME AND SCHOOL – *Writing Skills: Book A*

**Name:** _____

# My family

● Draw a picture of your family and write their names under the picture. Do not forget your pets.

_____

_____

_____

✎ **From the teacher**
Please read this sheet with your child. The activity helps children to remember to use capital letters at the beginning of names. It also helps them to recognise and write the names that they use frequently.

**To the teacher**

Signed: _____

Date: _____

**Name:** _____

# My friends

● Draw a picture of your friends and write their names under the picture.

_____

_____

**To the teacher**

Signed: _____

Date: _____

**Name:** _____

# My favourite food

● Label the foods below.

● I like this cereal.

_____

● I like these biscuits.

_____

● I like this drink.

● On the back of this sheet, draw and label three more foods that you like.

---

**From the teacher**
Please read this sheet with your child. Your child should complete the activity using 'product' names. They should use a capital letter at the beginning of each word.

**To the teacher**

Signed: _____

Date: _____

# Common words – Teachers' notes

## Introduction
*These activities:*
- *introduce a range of purposes for writing, for example for writing descriptions, lists, labels*
- *reinforce the concept that writing conveys a meaningful message that can be understood by other readers*
- *demonstrate the link between the spoken and the written word*
- *develop phonological awareness as the children increasingly associate letters with sounds of words.*

### Page 23 — All about me (Describing)

**Aim:** To provide children with the opportunity to compose a descriptive piece of writing about themselves.

**Activity:** This also demonstrates the skills of letter formation, spacing between words, the use of capital letters at the start of sentences and of full stops at the end.

### Page 24 — Label the body (Labelling body parts)

**Aim:** To recognise and write the names of parts of the body – important words for early reading and writing.

**Activity:** This also helps children to recognise the initial letters of words and to associate them with sounds. It could be linked to a class science topic on living things or to favourite class songs.

### Page 25 — My favourite clothes (Labelling clothes)

**Aim:** To recognise and write the names of the most common items of clothing.

**Activity:** This develops children's awareness of letters and sounds and consolidates the link between speaking, reading and writing. It could be linked with a class science topic on materials or a geographical topic on the seasons and the effects of weather, or to favourite books about clothes that have been shared in class.

### Page 26 — When I was a baby (Finishing sentences)

**Aim:** To associate spoken words with written ones and to reinforce understanding of the concept that writing carries a message.

**Activity:** This activity familiarises children with common words and the use of full stops. It can be linked to class topics on: change over time, growth, life cycles.

### Page 27 — What I can do (Lists)

**Aim:** To learn to write some of the most frequently used monosyllabic verbs.

**Activity:** This begins the process of building up a bank of known words that children can write on their own without copying. This will boost children's confidence in themselves as writers.

**Name:** _____

# All about me

● Draw a picture of yourself in the frame.
  Write about yourself, telling everyone what you look like.

_____

_____

_____

_____

**From the teacher**
Please read this sheet with your child. The activity helps children to make the connection between spoken and written words. Talk about colour, size, shape of features and style of hair, but let your child make the final decision about what to write. Encourage independence but be ready to help with the writing.

**To the teacher**

Signed: _____

Date: _____

**Name:** _____

# Label the body

● Write over the labels and draw arrows to the correct parts of the body.

hair

ears

eyes

nose

mouth

hands

arms

legs

feet

---

**From the teacher**
Please read this sheet with your child. The activity helps children to recognise and write the names of some parts of the body. Say each word with your child and help them draw arrows to the correct parts of the body.

**To the teacher**

Signed: _____

Date: _____

**Name:** _____

# My favourite clothes

● Draw yourself wearing your favourite clothes.
  Label the clothes.

**From the teacher**
Please read this sheet with your child. The activity helps children to
recognise and write the names of the most common items of
clothing. Help your child write the names of the items of clothing.

 **To the teacher**

Signed: _____

Date: _____

**Name:** _____

# When I was a baby

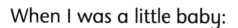

● Complete the list below.
Do not forget to put a full stop at
the end of each sentence.

When I was a little baby:

I used to crawl on the _____ *floor.* _____

I used to sleep in a _____

I used to eat with a _____

I used to sit in my _____

I used to smile at my _____

I used to ride in a _____

I used to cry when I was _____

I used to drink from a _____

 **From the teacher**
Please read this sheet with your child. The activity helps children to link commonly spoken words with written words. Explain the use of the full stop to your child and help him/her to use it.

**To the teacher**

Signed: _____

Date: _____

**Name:** _____

# What I can do

- Write a list of all the things you can do now. Do not forget to put a full stop at the end of each sentence.

I can _____     I can _____

I can _____     I can _____

I can _____     I can _____

- These words might help you.

jump    run    hop    skip

draw    paint    wash

**From the teacher**
Please read this sheet with your child. The activity helps children to write some common short verbs that they use frequently. This will boost their confidence in themselves as writers. Explain the use of the full stop to your child and help him/her to use it.

**To the teacher**

Signed: _____

Date: _____

# Writing for different purposes – Teachers' notes

## Introduction
*These activities:*
- *help to increase children's confidence through encouraging them to write about topics that are significant to them*
- *encourage them to recount specific memories*
- *encourage them to learn what appeals to an audience*
- *encourage them to use lively language patterns*
- *consolidate skills of left to right, top to bottom orientation on the page, capital letters, full stops, spacing between words and correct letter formation.*

*Many children will want an adult to write for them; some children will make their own marks on paper and a mixture of lower and upper cases will be common.*

---

### Page 29
### My favourite toy
### (Describing a toy)

**Aim:** To encourage children to talk, and then write about the toy that they like best.
**Activity:** If necessary, before sending the sheet home prompt the children with some ideas:
- What is the toy and what is special about it?
- How long have they had it?
- Who gave it to them, and when and where did they receive it?
- What do they do with it and who else plays with it?

---

### Page 30
### My top five
### (List, writing an account)

**Aim:** To encourage children to talk and write about television programmes.
**Activity:** If necessary, before sending the sheet home prompt the children with some ideas:
- What are the programmes and when are they on?
- What do they especially like about the programmes?
- Which are their favourite characters and why?
- What happened in their favourite episodes?
- What do they think might happen next?

---

### Page 31
### My school
### (Giving reasons)

**Aim:** To encourage children to talk and write about what they like about school.
**Activity:** If necessary, before sending the sheet home prompt the children with some ideas:
- What do they like best at school?
- What is special about their teacher?
- Who are their friends and what is special about them?
- What, if anything, do they worry about at school?
- Can they recall a special incident at school?

---

### Page 32
### A place I know
### (Recounting)

**Aim:** To encourage children to talk and write about the places they like to visit.
**Activity:** Discuss some of the different places the children might visit, such as the park, the funfair, a relative's house, the seaside, the shops, the swimming pool. Encourage them to consider:
- who they go/went with
- how they get/got there
- what happens/happened while they were there – what they did, saw, heard, smelt, felt, ate
- what makes/made the visit special.

---

### Page 33
### A time I remember
### (Writing about feelings)

**Aim:** To encourage children to talk and write about their experiences and feelings in different weather conditions.
**Activity:** Points to consider might be:
- the children's favourite weather and why
- what they wear in different weather conditions
- what they do/have done in the rain, snow, sun, wind
- a special occasion – where they went and who with.

HOME AND SCHOOL – *Writing Skills: Book A*

**Name:** _____

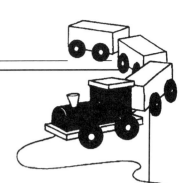

 # My favourite toy

- Draw your favourite toy.

- Now write about the toy.

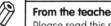 _____

_____

_____

_____

- Read your writing aloud.

---

✏️ **From the teacher**
Please read this sheet with your child. The activity helps children to feel confident about writing because the toy they choose is something that they know a lot about. It also develops general writing skills such as sentence structure. Encourage your child to talk about the colour and size of the toy, what it does and where it is played with. Be ready to help with the writing.

**To the teacher**

Signed: _____

Date: _____

**Name:**  _____

 # My top five

● Make a list of the programmes you like best on television.

1. _____

2. _____

3. _____

4. _____

5. _____

● Talk and write about one of the programmes.

_____

_____

_____

_____

_____

_____

● Now read your writing aloud.

**From the teacher**
Please read this sheet with your child. Writing about a subject that they know a lot about helps children to feel eager and confident. You should talk about when the programme is on, who watches with them, favourite characters, favourite episodes and what will happen next. Encourage independence but be ready to help with the writing.

**To the teacher**

Signed: _____

Date: _____

**Name:** _____

# My school

● Write down what you like best about school, saying why you like these things.

1. I like _____

   because _____

2. I like _____

   because _____

3. I like _____

   because _____

4. I like _____

   because _____

● Now read your writing aloud to make sure that you have not missed anything out.

 **From the teacher**
Please read this sheet with your child. Writing about a subject that
they know a lot about helps children feel eager and confident.
Discuss the information that will interest a reader, but let your child make the
decisions about what to write. Children should learn to give reasons using the
word 'because'. Be ready to help with the writing.

 **To the teacher**

Signed: _____

Date: _____

**Name:** _____

# A place I know

- Talk about a place you enjoy going to. Where is it? Who lives there? Who do you go with?
- Draw a picture and then write about a special visit there.

_____

_____

_____

_____

- Now read your writing aloud to make sure that you are happy with it.

**From the teacher**
Please read this sheet with your child. Writing about personal experiences that are significant in a child's life increases confidence and competence. Encourage independence but be ready to help with the writing.

**To the teacher**

Signed: _____

Date: _____

**Name:** _____

# A time I remember

- Talk about a special time you remember, that was in the rain, snow, sun or wind. What did you do? Who were you with? How did you feel?
- Draw a picture and then write about it.

_____

_____

_____

_____

- Now read your writing aloud to make sure that you have not missed anything out.

---

✏️ **From the teacher**
Please read this sheet with your child. Talk about a special occasion that occurred in a certain weather condition – rain, snow, sun or wind. Encourage your child to recount feelings as well as actions. If your child finds it difficult to write about a special time, write a couple of sentences for him/her to copy.

**To the teacher**

Signed: _____

Date: _____

# Writing to communicate – Teachers' notes

## Introduction

*These activities:*
- *extend the range of children's writing*
- *familiarise them with different organisational formats for writing, appropriate to the purpose and intended audience*

*Simple sentence structures with nouns and common verbs will predominate. Skills will be further consolidated as children will see in action, or use for themselves, left to right, top to bottom orientation on the page, capital letters, full stops, spacing between words and correct letter formation.*

*Many children will want an adult to write for them; some children will make their own marks on paper and a mixture of lower- and upper-case letters will be common. Reliance on the initial sounds of words is to be expected.*

---

### Page 35 — The lunch box (Labelling)

**Aim:** To introduce children to writing as a means of labelling articles.

**Activity:** There is little writing to be done here so prior discussion of the items and of children's views about favourite foods, healthy foods, who makes their packed lunches, who has school dinners, etc is a crucial part of the learning. Talking before writing also enables children to match spoken and written words as well as helping them to clarify their thoughts.

---

### Page 36 — A special message (Writing a message)

**Aim:** For children to talk about and then write a message to someone very special – their teacher!

**Activity:** The activity helps children to learn to express feelings on paper. This is a vital step in the learning process. They will develop an understanding that writing has a permanence which a spoken message has not.

---

### Page 37 — Going shopping (Lists)

**Aim:** To familiarise children with the conventions of writing a list and sorting items into categories.

**Activity:** The children are asked to write out their shopping list in categories that will mirror a real-life situation. The activity will help them to recognise and write commonly used words and will help develop their phonological awareness.

It may be useful to talk about favourite foods, where the children go shopping, who with, how often etc.

---

### Page 38 — Thank you (Writing a note)

**Aim:** To introduce children to the format and the appropriate language for writing a short thank-you note.

**Activity:** Encourage children to reflect on how important it is to offer thanks to people for their kindness. Remind them how much we all like to feel valued by someone.

---

### Page 39 — Greetings card (Designing a card)

**Aim:** To introduce children to the format, language and illustrations of a greetings card.

**Activity:** Discuss with the children:
- who they want to send the card to
- what occasion they want to celebrate
- what they want to say (depending on the occasion decided upon)
- how to say it appropriately (depending on the age, gender and relationship of the recipient)
- how to decorate the card.

Name: _____

# The lunch box

● Look carefully at the pictures of food in the lunch box and at the labels below.
Talk about the different foods and then write the correct label near each picture. Draw a line from the label to the correct food.

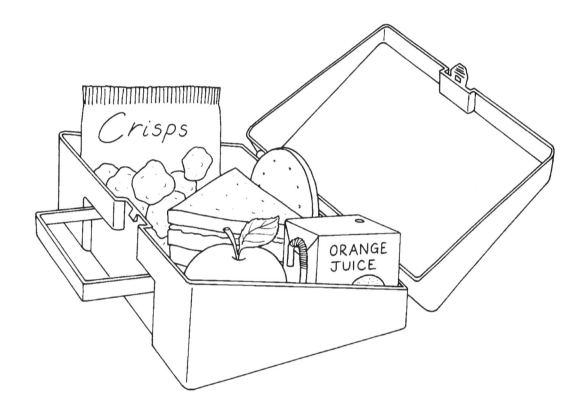

| a sandwich | an apple | a biscuit |

| a drink | a bag of crisps |

**From the teacher**
Please read this sheet with your child. The activity helps to broaden children's experience of writing for different purposes and in different formats. Remember that talking before writing will help your child to match spoken and written words. It will also help your child to clarify his/her thoughts.

**To the teacher**

Signed: _____

Date: _____

**Name:** _____

# A special message

● Write a message to your teacher to explain how special he/she is.

Dear _____

I am glad you are my teacher

because _____

_____

_____

_____

Love from _____

---

**From the teacher**
Please read this sheet with your child. The activity introduces children to the format for writing a brief message and helps to develop skills in communicating feelings in writing.

**To the teacher**

Signed: _____

Date: _____

**Name:** _____

# Going shopping

- Here is a list of foods. Talk about which shop you would visit to buy each thing.
  Write each thing on the correct list below.

| | |
|---|---|
| apples | chicken |
| bananas | crisps |
| beef | jam |
| biscuits | pears |
| rice | potatoes |
| butter | sugar |
| carrots | sausages |

Fruit and vegetable shop

Butcher's shop

Grocery shop

 **From the teacher**
Please read this sheet with your child. The activity introduces children to writing lists and to sorting items into categories. Have fun talking about your family's favourite food items and your weekly shopping sprees.

**To the teacher**

Signed: _____

Date: _____

**Name:** _____

# Thank you

● Writing to say thank you is a very important job. There are all sorts of reasons for saying thank you – you might want to thank someone for giving you a present, for helping you or visiting you when you were sick. Think of someone who has been kind to you recently and write a note to let them know how pleased you were.

Thank You

*Dear* _____

*Thank you very much for*

_____

_____

_____

_____

_____

_____

*From* _____

**From the teacher**
Please read this sheet with your child. The activity introduces children to an appropriate format for writing a thank-you note. Encourage your child to make the decisions about what has to be included but be ready to help with the writing.

**To the teacher**

Signed: _____

Date: _____

**Name:** _____

# Greetings card

● Design a greetings card for a special occasion.

---

✏️ **From the teacher**
Please read this sheet with your child. The activity introduces children to designing a greetings card. Before you start, talk about what to write and how to decorate the card to make it look attractive.

**To the teacher**

Signed: _____

Date: _____

---

# Linking reading and writing – Teachers' notes

## Introduction

*These activities:*
- *help children to understand the close links between reading and writing*
- *further familiarise children with the conventions of book language, traditional story beginnings, and endings*
- *provide an opportunity to respond to the rhymes and rhythms of the English language*
- *develop children's understanding of writing as a means of remembering*
- *provide ongoing opportunities to develop key writing skills, for example phonological awareness, sequencing of ideas and fluid handwriting movements.*

*Many children will want an adult to write for them and some will want to copy the writing afterwards; some children will make their own marks on paper and a mixture of lower- and upper-case letters will be common. Reliance on the initial sounds of words is to be expected. Encourage the children to find the names of characters from books.*

### Page 41 — The lost kitten (Sequencing)

**Aim:** To develop the children's sequencing skills and further their development as writers.
**Activity:** The children are asked to order a set of pictures and supply text to create a narrative. They should draw on their knowledge of narrative structure.

### Page 42 — Let's make pancakes (Action rhymes)

**Aim:** To enhance children's recognition of rhyme and rhythm. This helps to develop children's phonological awareness.
**Activity:** The children are asked to recite and complete a well-known action rhyme and to write lists of rhyming words. Point out the similarity of the letter strings in rhyming word endings.

### Page 43 — Nursery rhyme riddles (Recognising rhymes)

**Aims:** The activity helps children to:
- link reading and writing
- recall events from well-known nursery rhymes
- recognise and write rhyming words
- use capital letters for people's names.

**Activity:** The children are asked to write lists of rhyming words and then to play with language in a creative way, using the rhyming words from their lists.

### Page 44 — Fairy tales (Matching words to pictures)

**Aims:**
- To encourage children to read for meaning.
- To reinforce the rhymes and rhythms of the English language.

**Activity:** Discuss possible options before the children match the captions to the pictures. The children also have to provide a title for each set, drawing on their prior knowledge of traditional stories. Sharing the children's work in class provides an opportunity for them to justify their choices.

### Page 45 — Fun with fairy tales (Recalling events)

**Aims:**
- To link reading and writing.
- To help children to recall events from fairy stories.
- To read for meaning and make deductions.
- To highlight the traditional story opener 'Once upon a time'.
- To reinforce the use of capital letters for people's names.

**Activity:** The children are asked to complete sentences using well-known characters' names. Help the children to recall favourite fairy tales and name the characters in them.

**Name:** _____

# The lost kitten

- Look at the pictures and number them 1, 2, 3, 4, in the order that you think makes the best story.

- On the back of this sheet, write a story to accompany the pictures.

**From the teacher**
Read this sheet with your child. The activity helps to develop children's ability to sequence events and create text to match a set of pictures. Offer and talk about ideas for an imaginative story. Help your child with his/her writing where necessary.

**To the teacher**

Signed: _____

Date: _____

**Name:** _____

# Let's make pancakes

● Read the rhyme and fill in the missing rhyming word:

Stir the pancake, beat the pancake,

Pop it in the pan.

Fry the pancake, toss the pancake,

Catch it if you __ __ __.

● Think of as many words as you can that rhyme with **pan** and write them below.

**pan** _____  _____  _____

_____  _____  _____

_____  _____  _____

● Now think of some words that rhyme with **pop**.

**pop** _____  _____  _____

_____  _____  _____

_____  _____  _____

---

✎ **From the teacher**
Please read this sheet with your child. The activity helps children to recognise and supply rhyming words. It also reinforces the link between reading and writing. Help your child to find as many rhyming words as they can.

**To the teacher**

Signed: _____

Date: _____

**Name:** _____

# Nursery rhyme riddles

● Read the questions about nursery rhyme characters and write the answers in the spaces.

1. Who went up the hill? _____

2. Who lost her sheep? _____

3. Who sat on a tuffet? _____

4. Who sat in the corner? _____

5. Who was a merry old soul? _____

6. Who went to her cupboard? _____

7. Who went to Gloucester? _____

8. Who sat among the cinders? _____

● Make a list of other words that rhyme with:

| **sheep** | **soul** | **hill** |
| --- | --- | --- |
| _____ | _____ | _____ |
| _____ | _____ | _____ |
| _____ | _____ | _____ |
| _____ | _____ | _____ |

● Now make up some silly sentences using words from your list. Here is one to get you started: The sleeping sheep keep weeping!

✎ **From the teacher**
Please read this sheet with your child. The activity helps children to recall well-known rhymes, to read for meaning and to recognise and supply rhyming words. Remind your child to use capital letters for the names of people. Encourage your child to spot the rhyming patterns in the nursery rhymes (hill – Jill, sheep – peep).

**To the teacher**

Signed: _____

Date: _____

**Name:** _____

# Fairy tales

● Look carefully at the pictures and read the captions.
  Cut out the captions and stick them under the correct pictures.
  Write the title of each fairy tale in the space at the top of
  each picture.

"I'll huff and I'll puff
And I'll blow your house down!"

"Fee fi fo fum,
I smell the blood of an Englishman."

"Run, run, as fast as you can,
You can't catch me,
I'm the gingerbread man!"

"Oh Grandmama, what big ears you have!"
"All the better to hear you with, my dear."

**From the teacher**
Please read this sheet with your child. The activity helps children to read for meaning and match words to pictures.
Help your child to write the title of each fairy story.

**Name:** _____

# Fun with fairy tales

● Read the sentences carefully and fill in the gaps with the names of the correct fairy tale characters.

1. Once upon a time there were three _____

   _____ .

2. Once upon a time _____ lived with her two ugly

   sisters.

3. Once upon a time _____ found a magic lamp in

   a cave.

4. Once upon a time _____ _____

   lived in the woods with seven _____ .

5. Once upon a time _____ _____

   pricked her finger and fell asleep for a hundred years.

● Make up three more sentences for your friends at school to solve. Remember to start with 'Once upon a time'.

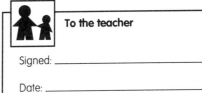

1. _____ _____

2. _____

3. _____

**From the teacher**
Please read this sheet with your child. The activity helps children to recall events from well-known fairy stories, to read for meaning and make deductions. It also highlights the traditional story opening 'Once upon a time'. Encourage your child to use capital letters for the names of people.

**To the teacher**

Signed: _____

Date: _____

# My homework diary

Name _____

---

### Advice about homework

Your child will gain more from the homework activity if you spend time giving support and encouragement.

- It is better for your child to do a little well than to do a lot carelessly.
- Pleasure and confidence are the keys to success.
- If your child is worried about a homework activity, please contact the teacher.

***REMEMBER:*** all learners need praise and encouragement.

HOME AND SCHOOL – *Writing Skills: Book A*

Name of activity _____

What I enjoyed most _____

What I found difficult _____

Parent/carer comment _____

Signed _____ Date _____

---

Name of activity _____

What I enjoyed most _____

What I found difficult _____

Parent/carer comment _____

Signed _____ Date _____

# Teachers' Guide: Home and School – Writing Skills

| | Handwriting | Spelling | Punctuation | Language/Grammar | Types of writing |
|---|---|---|---|---|---|
| **Book 1** | Patterns<br>Lower-case letters | Letter sounds<br>Rhymes and rhythm | Full stops,<br>capital letters | Capital letters<br>Simple sentences<br>Subject–verb<br>agreement | Descriptions<br>Labels<br>Lists<br>Letters<br>Messages |
| **Book 2** | Revision<br>Ascenders and<br>descenders | Initial sounds<br>Digraphs and blends<br>Onset and rime<br>Word patterns | Full stops<br>Capital letters<br>Question marks | Language changes<br>Bi and tri<br>Similes<br>Sentence structure<br>Vocabulary | Stories, Comics<br>Diary<br>Postcard<br>Letter<br>Notice<br>Invitation<br>Posters<br>Writing to persuade<br>Writing to describe |
| **Book 3** | Baseline joins<br>Top and middle joins<br>Reverse joins<br>High-frequency words | Prefix: un<br>Suffixes: ful, less, ing,<br>ed<br>Double consonants | Full stops<br>Capital letters<br>Speech bubbles<br>Thought bubbles<br>Commas<br>Exclamation marks | Alliteration<br>Adjectives<br>Expressive verbs | Book review<br>Crosswords<br>Newspaper articles<br>Report<br>Speech<br>Non-fiction writing<br>Narrative writing |